Comets, Meteors, Asteroids, and the Outer Reaches

TRUDY E. BELL

To the middle-schoolers of Messiah Lutheran School, especially my beloved Roxana

—T.E.B.

Published by Smart Apple Media, 1980 Lookout Drive, North Mankato, Minnesota 56003

Photo credits: Page 4: copyright © 2003 Chris Butler. Page 6, 7: courtesy NASA. Page 8: copyright © 2003 Fran Bagenal. Page 9 (top): courtesy NASA. Page 9 (bottom): copyright © 2003 Pat Rawlings/NASA/JPL. Page 11: copyright © 2003 Fran Bagenal. Page 12: copyright © 2003 Marc Buie/Lowell Observatory. Page 14: courtesy NASA. Page 15: © 2003 Mansell. Page 17: Courtesy of the Lakeview Historical Society/Mrs. Marie Fults. Page 18: copyright © 2003 John Laborde. Page 19, 20: courtesy NASA. Page 23: copyright © 2003 Calvin J. Hamilton. Page 25: courtesy NASA. Page 26: courtesy NASA. Page 27: courtesy NASA/Don Davis. Page 28: copyright © 2003 Tony Hallas. Page 29: copyright © 2003 Jerry Lodrifus. Page 31: courtesy NASA. Page 32: copyright © 2003 Pierre Thomas. Page 33: Meteor Crater, Northern Arizona, USA. Page 34: copyright © 2003 Sigurour H. Stefnisson. Page 36: copyright © 2003 Steve Albers. Page 37: copyright © 2003 J. Watanabe. Page 39: copyright © 2003 Dr. Herbert Kroehl, NGDC. Page 40: copyright © 2003 David Talent/NOAO/AURA/NSF. Page 41: copyright © 2003 Steve Albers. Page 45: copyright © 2003 Juan Carlos Casado/Skylook.net.
Cover art © 2003 Chris Butler.

Library of Congress Cataloging-in-Publication Data

Bell, Trudy E.
Comets, meteors, asteroids, and the outer reaches / by Trudy E. Bell.
p. cm. — (The new solar system)
Summary: Explores the solar system's smallest bodies and outer reaches to seek information about some unusual objects and how they may affect life on Earth. Includes bibliographical references.
Contents: Pluto and Charon: more questions than answers — Comets: 'The nearest thing to nothing' — Asteroids: danger from space? — Shooting stars and fireballs — Dust, particles, fields, and cosmic light shows — Watching the fireworks of heaven.
ISBN 1-58340-289-6
1. Astronomy—Juvenile literature. [1. Astronomy. 2. Solar System.] I. Title. II. Series.
QB46.B425 2003   523.2—dc21   2003043433

First Edition

9 8 7 6 5 4 3 2 1

Contents

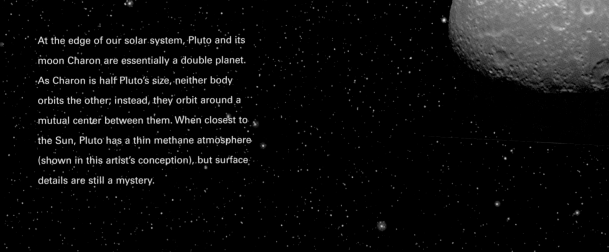

At the edge of our solar system, Pluto and its moon Charon are essentially a double planet. As Charon is half Pluto's size, neither body orbits the other; instead, they orbit around a mutual center between them. When closest to the Sun, Pluto has a thin methane atmosphere (shown in this artist's conception), but surface details are still a mystery.

Smallest Bodies, Spectacular Displays

Size isn't everything in the solar system. Sure, the Sun and Jupiter together account for more than 99 percent of the solar system's mass and thus throw their weight around by controlling the orbits of the planets, their moons, and every other body large and small.

But some of the most spectacular visual shows in the heavens are staged by the solar system's tiniest objects: chunks of ice, grains of sand, and even fragments of atoms. For example, every few years a ghostly comet swoops in toward the Sun, growing a tail millions of miles long that may stretch halfway across the star-spangled sky just before dawn or after sunset—and this show originates from a dirty ball of ice only a few miles across. Several times each year, "falling stars" rain through the nighttime sky as Earth moves through streams of sand and gravel—tiny shards of long-dead comets. During winters in far northern or southern latitudes, the night sky dances with silent green and red curtains—the auroras, produced when charged subatomic particles from the Sun interact with Earth's magnetic field and upper atmosphere.

If you were to hitch a ride on a visiting comet and accompany it back to the cradle of its birth, you would find yourself in the dim deep freeze of the outer solar system beyond Neptune, which is as yet unseen by any spacecraft. The distant ninth planet Pluto is a mysterious body, its seasons so chill that for half its year its very atmosphere freezes and blankets its surface. Indeed, debates rage about whether Pluto with its satellite Charon is more properly a double planet—or whether it's even a planet at all. Pluto may be cold, but it's certainly not lonely, as it's kept company by more than 100 smaller and very strange worldlets in silent, eccentric (elliptical) orbits.

Come explore the bizarre, the mysterious, and the unexpected. This is the veritable Antarctica of the solar system: its remote outer reaches and smallest bodies.

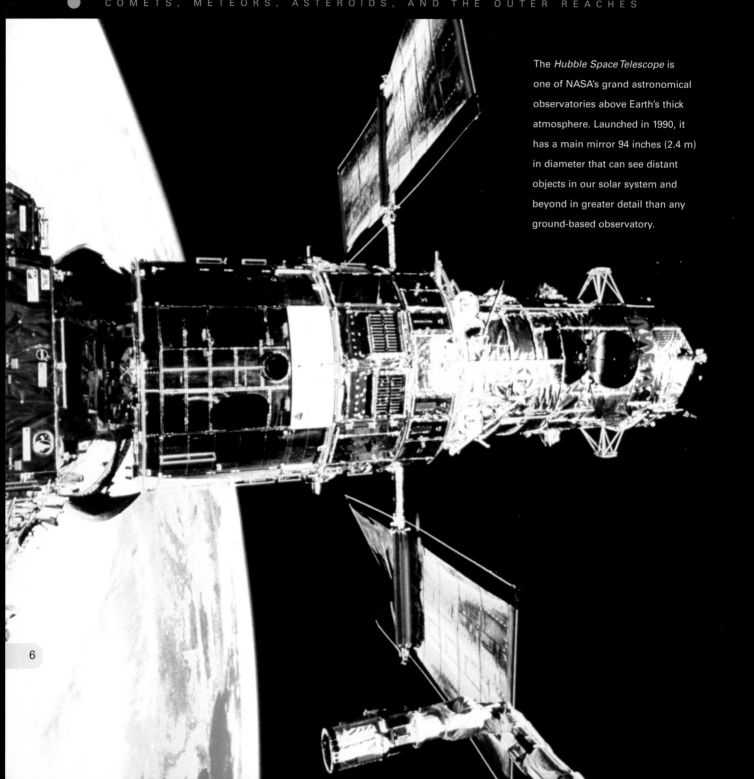

The *Hubble Space Telescope* is one of NASA's grand astronomical observatories above Earth's thick atmosphere. Launched in 1990, it has a main mirror 94 inches (2.4 m) in diameter that can see distant objects in our solar system and beyond in greater detail than any ground-based observatory.

Pluto and Charon: More Questions than Answers

Pluto is so remote that sunlight, which takes only eight minutes to get from the Sun to Earth, needs nearly four hours to reach Pluto. And Pluto is so tiny and dim that surface details eluded astronomers until the launch of the *Hubble Space Telescope* above Earth's atmosphere. Pluto remains the only planet not yet visited by any spacecraft. Most of what we know comes from extraordinarily clever astronomical sleuthing from Earth—and there are still far more questions than answers.

One of the first oddities astronomers noticed about Pluto is its peculiar orbit. The other eight planets all have orbits that lie roughly in the plane of the Sun's equator and that are more or less circular. The plane of Pluto's orbit, however, is tilted at a completely cockeyed angle. Even weirder, its orbit is so eccentric that for part of each Plutonian year, the ninth planet is more than 50 times as far from the Sun as Earth, while half a Plutonian year later it's only 30 Earth distances away from the Sun. Indeed, Pluto actually spends 20 years of its 248-Earth-year-long year as the *eighth* planet, closer to the Sun than Neptune—most recently from 1979 to 1999. Pluto will become the eighth planet again in September 2226.

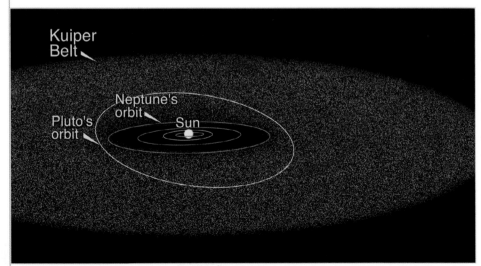

The orbit of the ninth planet Pluto is tilted at a much steeper angle than the orbit of any other planets in the solar system. Even stranger, Pluto's orbit sometimes carries the planet closer to the Sun than the eighth planet Neptune! Pluto and Charon also lie in the Kuiper belt, a distant realm of small icy bodies.

Another oddity is the fact that Pluto appears to interrupt a pronounced pattern in the solar system. The four planets closest to the Sun (Mercury, Venus, Earth, and Mars)—the so-called terrestrial planets—are much like Earth in being small, rocky, and dense. The next four planets (Jupiter, Saturn, Uranus, and Neptune) are all massive, bloated gas giants. And then there's distant Pluto—small, rocky, and dense. What's going on? That question still has astronomers scratching their heads, because any theory about the formation and evolution of the solar system must account for this peculiarity.

For nearly half a century after Pluto's discovery in 1930, astronomers had only the vaguest idea about the ninth planet's size and mass and no decent view of its possible surface features. Then they got unexpectedly lucky. In 1978 an astronomer named James Christy discovered that Pluto's light seemed to be dimming and brightening every 6.4 days. He soon realized that Pluto had a satellite—and a big one compared to the planet. Moreover, the orbits of Pluto and Earth lined up a few years later in 1985 so that the satellite was regularly eclipsing parts of Pluto as seen from Earth. Not only did the satellite, which Christy named Charon, let astronomers determine Pluto's actual size and mass, but the exact pattern of dimming and brightening allowed them to map dark and light features on its surface.

If we were to visit Pluto, what would we find?

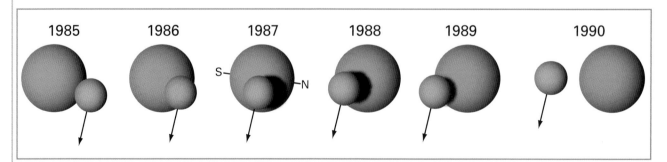

From 1985 through 1990, the plane of Charon's orbit around Pluto happened to line up with Earth and astronomers were able to see Pluto and Charon eclipsing each other. By timing those mutual eclipses, astronomers were able to calculate Pluto's and Charon's sizes.

Pluto, the farthest planet from the Sun, and its moon Charon are clearly shown as being two distinct objects in this image captured by the *Hubble Space Telescope* on February 21, 1994, when Pluto was 2.6 billion miles (4.4 billion km) from Earth—some 30 times farther than Earth is from the Sun. A bright highlight on Pluto (the larger disk) suggests it has a smooth, reflective surface layer. (Image is not shown to scale.)

Although no spacecraft has visited Pluto and Charon, from what we've learned from closeup images of other planets and moons in the solar system, an artist has created this rendition.

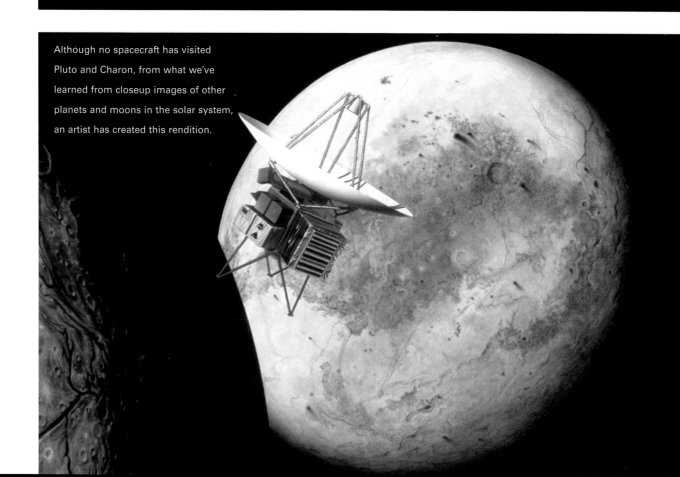

9

First, it's mighty dim out there, especially during Plutonian winter. The Sun would appear as a brilliant but tiny point of light, about the size of the planet Venus seen at sunrise or sunset on Earth as the morning or evening star. When Pluto's highly elliptical orbit brings it within the orbit of Neptune, the Sun would be about 1/900 as bright as it is on Earth, but when Pluto's orbit carries it farthest away, the Sun would be only 1/2,500 as bright—casting little more light than the full Moon does on Earth.

Second, seasons on Pluto are extreme. On Earth (and Mars), seasons occur mainly because the planet's axis of rotation is tilted about 23 degrees with respect to the plane of its orbit. Thus, for a quarter of the year, the sun is high in the southern sky (giving rise to southern summer and northern winter), and for another quarter, it's high in the northern sky (giving rise to northern summer and southern winter); the rest of the year it's high over the equator (giving rise to spring and fall in both hemispheres). Pluto's axis of rotation, however, practically lies in the plane of its orbit—similar to the case of Uranus—so during some parts of its year, its south or north pole is pointing almost directly at the Sun. If that were the case on Earth, the tropics would extend to the Arctic and the Antarctic! So Pluto should have a bizarre climate.

It does, but less because of the extreme tilt of its axis than because of its highly elliptical orbit. When Pluto is closer to the Sun than Neptune, it warms up enough to be blanketed with a gaseous atmosphere—a thin one, to be sure (only 1/100,000 the density of Earth's), but nonetheless a real atmosphere. But as Pluto recedes from the Sun, its atmosphere gradually freezes and falls to the frigid ground like frost. Winter there is not only wickedly cold but very, very long, as one Plutonian year lasts nearly two and a half Earth centuries.

Third, Pluto's relationship with its satellite Charon is unique in the solar system. Charon is very close to Pluto—only 12,200 miles (19,600 km) away, about 1/20 the distance of the Moon from Earth. At about 750 miles (1,200 km) in diameter, Charon is about half the size of Pluto (1,500 miles

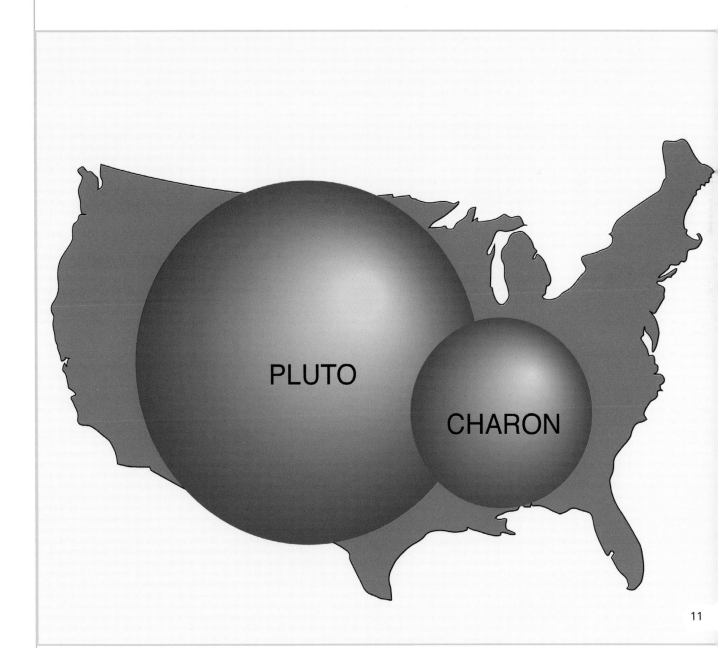

Placed side by side, Pluto and Charon are still collectively smaller than the width of the United States.

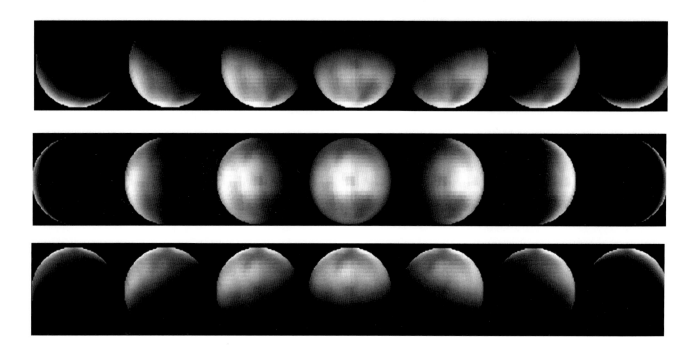

Charon's Phases

As seen from Pluto, Charon would go through a very unusual sequence of phases compared to the Moon as seen from Earth. To understand why, you need to know four things. First, unlike Earth, Pluto rotates "on its side"—its axis of rotation lies nearly in the plane of its orbit around the Sun; as a result, it has very pronounced seasons. Second, Pluto orbits the Sun very slowly, one Plutonian year being about 248 Earth years, so seasons are also very long. Third, Charon orbits around Pluto in Pluto's equatorial plane, almost perpendicular to Pluto's orbit around the Sun; also, Charon's orbital period is the same as one Plutonian day: 6.4 Earth days. Fourth, because one side of Pluto always faces Charon and vice versa, Charon would appear to hang in one spot in the sky going through a complete set of phases each Plutonian day. But no two sets of phases would be alike! What would you see?

When Pluto was discovered in 1930, it was just before the start of winter in Pluto's northern hemisphere; the Sun would pass overhead at 53 degrees south latitude (about equivalent to the tip of South America on Earth). So Charon's phases would look like the top row. In 1988, the Sun was overhead at Pluto's equator, marking the beginning of spring in the northern hemisphere, and full moon Charon was really full (second row); solar and lunar eclipses would have occurred every Plutonian day for six years. The year 2030 will be the start of summer in Pluto's northern hemisphere, when the Sun will pass overhead at 56 degrees north latitude (equivalent to Scotland on Earth), and Charon's phases will look like the third row.

[2400 km] in diameter); by comparison, the Moon is only a quarter the diameter of Earth. Thus Pluto and Charon seem more like a double planet than a planet and satellite. But the two bodies are so different from each other that astronomers doubt they formed at the same time. Pluto is dense enough to be mostly rock covered with ices of nitrogen, methane, ethane, and carbon monoxide, while Charon appears to be made mostly of water ice.

Charon orbits Pluto in 6.4 days. But Pluto also rotates once on its axis in 6.4 days. In other words, Charon's orbital period is equal to Pluto's day. That means Charon is in a synchronous orbit around Pluto, just like communications satellites around Earth. Not only does Charon keep one face toward Pluto (as the Moon does Earth), but Pluto also keeps only one face toward Charon. Thus, from half of Pluto, Charon is always hanging in just one position in the sky while going through a complete set of Moon-like phases in less than a week; from the other half of Pluto, Charon would never be visible at all.

As distant as Pluto and Charon are from the Sun, they are not alone. Indeed, they appear to be but the largest bodies in the mysterious Kuiper belt, a donut-shaped region of small icy objects beyond the orbit of Neptune. Astronomers estimate that there may be more than 35,000 Kuiper belt objects larger than 60 miles (100 km) in diameter in orbit roughly 30 to 100 times as far as the Earth is from the Sun.

Comets can and do still strike planets today. In fact, between July 16 and 22, 1994, astronomers watched in fascination as 21 fragments of Comet Shoemaker-Levy 9 (shown in this artist's rendering as a "string of pearls") plowed into the southern hemisphere of Jupiter on the planet's unseen far side.

Comets: "The Nearest Thing to Nothing..."

They come seemingly from nowhere. They hang in the evening or morning sky for a few weeks. And then they slowly disappear, mute, ghostly, spine-tingling. From antiquity through the 17th century, they were feared as sources of plagues or taken as signs from God, often likened to His sword hanging in the sky as a warning to His disobedient people.

What are these apparitions of awe-inspiring beauty?

They are comets—some of the smallest yet flashiest bodies in the solar system.

Although early observers thought comets were "exhalations" of Earth's atmosphere, Johannes Kepler, Galileo Galilei, and Sir Isaac Newton suspected they were of celestial origin. Indeed, that comets are bodies in our solar system was dramatically proven by British astronomer Edmund Halley. After poring over historical observations of comets, he hypothesized that certain bright comets seen about every 76 years were actually just *one* object revolving around the Sun in a 76-year orbit. After he accurately predicted the comet's return between late 1758 (when it was first sighted on Christmas Day) and early 1759, it became the most famous comet known: Halley's comet.

Englishman Isaac Newton (1642–1727, above shown investigating the various properties of light) quantified how gravity controls the motions of bodies orbiting one another.

Why choose the name "433 Eros" for an asteroid? Why "Shoemaker-Levy 9" for a comet?

When children are about to be born, perhaps their parents consult books of children's names and their meanings. Well, since 1919 astronomers have consulted the International Astronomical Union (IAU) for rules about naming solar system objects.

When an observer first discovers an asteroid (new ones are being found every month), he or she notifies the IAU, which gives it a temporary designation. Once its orbit has been reliably determined, which could take several years, it's given a permanent number. Eros, for example, is number 433 (the number now used tops 5,000). The person determining the new asteroid's orbit, who may be someone different from its discoverer, also can propose a name that must be no more than 16 characters long, not too similar to the name of another asteroid or planet's moon. Asteroids have even been named after rock stars Ringo Starr and Eric Clapton!

Naming comets used to be simple. The first comet that became known by someone's name is famous Halley's comet (Halley has a short "a," rhyming with "alley"), because Edmund Halley was the first to realize that the comets seen in 1607 and 1682 were the same object, leading him to predict its return again in early 1759. Eventually, comets came to be named after their discoverers, and then numbered if the same two observers simultaneously discovered others: for example, Shoemaker-Levy 9 was the ninth comet co-discovered by Eugene Shoemaker and David Levy.

By 1995, however, there was so much confusion among names that the IAU revised the system. Now comets just get letters and numbers describing the type of comet, the year of observation, the first half-month of discovery, and the discovery sequence. Shoemaker-Levy 9 was officially redesignated D/1993 F2 (D meaning it died when it hit Jupiter, it was first seen in 1993 in late March, and it was the second comet discovered in 1993).

Now comets are known to be mountain-sized, dirty snowballs or icy mud balls—a mixture of ices (water ice and frozen smelly gases such as methane and ammonia) and dust that for some reason never coalesced into planets when the solar system was formed nearly five billion years ago. Thus, comets are samples of the most ancient materials in the solar system.

Most of the time, these grubby icebergs reside in the cold, dark outer reaches of the solar system beyond Neptune. But occasionally, lured by the gravitational pull of Jupiter or some other body, one starts to fall inward toward the Sun. And that's when the show begins.

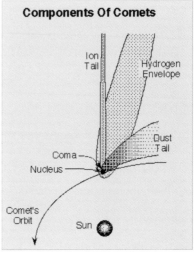

Components Of Comets

Comets are composed of five distinct parts. The comet's head is composed of the bright, starlike "nucleus" surrounded by a fuzzy, gaseous coma. As a comet approaches the Sun, chemical reactions release hydrogen gas, which then surrounds the comet in a huge hydrogen envelope. The Sun's heat also drives off dust and gas from the nucleus, creating the comet's curved, yellowish-white dust tail and straight bluish ion tail.

Halley's comet, perhaps the most famous comet of all time, was photographed in 1910 over Lake Erie in Lakeview, Ohio. During this spectacular appearance, the comet approached so close that Earth actually passed through its tail!

Somewhere outside the orbit of Mars, the Sun's heat is strong enough that the ball of dirty ice starts sizzling and outgassing, forming a fuzzy tail. As it grows larger and brighter over passing weeks, it displays five distinct parts. Brightest is the starlike "nucleus"—the dirty snowball itself, typically less than six miles (10 km) across, that is the source of the entire display. Surrounding the nucleus is a fuzzy-looking, gaseous "coma," a dense cloud of water, carbon dioxide, and other neutral gases sublimed (directly evaporated from solid into gas) from the nucleus. The coma and nucleus together form the comet's head.

As the comet moves even closer to the Sun, solar ultraviolet radiation (the rays that cause sunburn) causes chemical reactions in the nucleus that release hydrogen gas, which surrounds the comet in a huge hydrogen envelope millions of miles in diameter. Because ultraviolet radiation is absorbed by Earth's atmosphere, the enormous hydrogen envelope can't be seen from the ground, but it has been detected from spacecraft.

Even more dramatically, the Sun's heat drives off gas and dust from the nucleus, creating the comet's long tails. Most comets have two distinct tails. Most prominent is its curved, whitish or yellowish dust tail; up to five or six million miles (8–10 million km) long, it is composed of smoke-sized particles of dust blown off the nucleus by escaping gases. As insubstantial as the microscopic dust motes are, they still have mass. Each

17

Comet West, here photographed on March 9, 1976, was a bright, ghostly object that could be seen just before dawn almost due east.

particle is in its own individual orbit around the Sun and is accelerated slowly by solar radiation pressure. Thus, a comet's dust tail looks—and really is—curved.

Fainter but much longer is the comet's ion tail: up to several hundred million miles long and extending virtually straight away from the Sun, the bluish ion tail is composed of charged subatomic particles of gases and may be laced with rays and streamers from the solar wind. In this way, a humble ball of ice only walking distance across can create a bright, beautiful tail longer than the distance from the Sun to Earth. Indeed, a writer for *National Geographic* called comets "the nearest thing to nothing anything can be and still be something."

The closer to the Sun a comet falls, the more the ices heat and evaporate, and the more spectacular the display. Some comets—known as sun-grazers—have come to within less than the Sun's own radius of the Sun's searing face, whipping around the Sun in a celestial crack-the-whip so violent that the nucleus has been wrenched apart into several pieces.

For a few weeks just before and after perihelion (the comet's closest approach to the Sun), the comet is brightest and most beautiful. Then, as it recedes into the colder, outer reaches of the solar system, its tails shorten, fade, and eventually disappear. Within months, the comet is beyond sight of any Earth-based telescope.

Where do comets come from? And where do they go after their marvelous display?

By studying comets' orbits, astronomers have long known that comets are residents of our solar system rather than from the space between the stars and galaxies. But their orbits also indicate that comets seem to have at least two very different homes.

Short-period comets—ones that like Halley's comet return again and again, every 3 to 200 years—have orbits more or less in the same plane as the planets. They are believed to spend most of their time in the Kuiper belt beyond Neptune, keeping company with Pluto and Charon.

Long-period comets—ones that may return only after centuries or millennia—often have orbits steeply inclined to the plane of the planets. Some even may be entering the inner solar system for the very first time. They are believed to reside in the far more distant spherical Oort cloud, whose most distant reaches are believed to extend hundreds or thousands of times farther than Pluto, perhaps even 1/10 of the way to the nearest star. Since the Oort cloud is still bound by the Sun's gravity, it is clear that the solar system is truly immense (sunlight would take about two months to reach the outer edge of the Oort cloud).

As comets have such eccentric orbits, do they ever hit planets? Definitely yes! In 1994 the world's astronomers watched from ground-based observatories and the *Hubble Space Telescope* as comet Shoemaker-Levy 9 broke into 21 fragments that between July 16 and 22 plowed into the atmosphere of the planet Jupiter. It was the first time such a celestial event was ever witnessed.

Even vaster than the disk-shaped Kuiper belt is the spherical Oort cloud, comprised of billions of comets. Its farthest reaches are believed to extend hundreds or thousands of times farther from the Sun than Pluto.

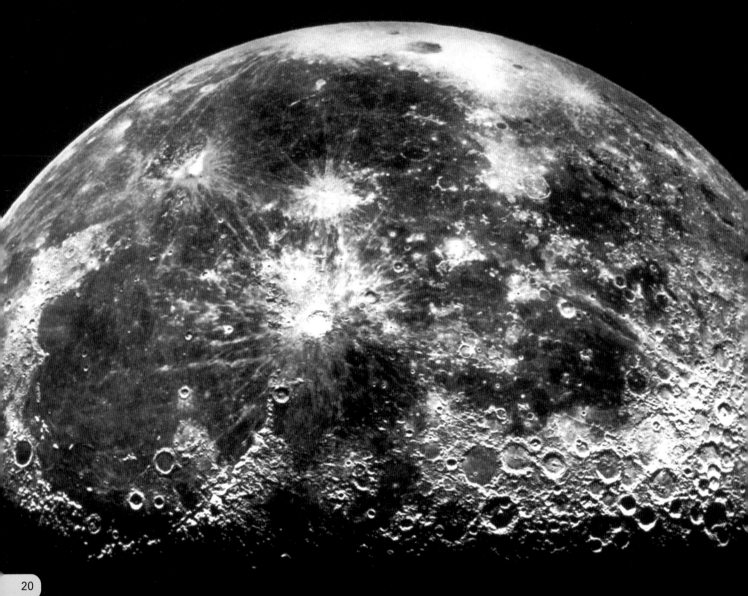

The Moon is pitted with craters, many of which were excavated
by rocky chunks of interplanetary debris bombarding the surface.
Some craters are so ancient they date back to the early days of
the solar system's formation.

CHAPTER THREE

Asteroids: Danger from Space?

Take a look at the Moon through binoculars or a small telescope. Its face is pockmarked with thousands of craters, both large and small. Astronomically speaking, Earth is the Moon's next-door neighbor—and also a much bigger target. Why don't we see thousands of craters on Earth?

As the solar system was forming some 4.5 billion years ago, both Earth and the Moon were bombarded with asteroids—chunks of rock and iron tens or even hundreds of miles across that never formed into planets. But Earth is geologically very active, with volcanoes spewing lava and crustal plates grinding together to raise up mountains. Moreover, unlike the Moon, Earth is climatologically very active, with rain, sandstorms, floods, and glaciers wearing down its surface—not to mention the action of tree and plant roots slowly crushing rocks into fertile soil. As a result, while some of the Moon's visible surface is nearly as ancient as the solar system, most of Earth's visible surface has been recycled several times and is less than one billion years old, so evidence of the earliest craters has long since been erased.

Nonetheless, geologists have identified at least 160 impact craters on Earth up to 100 miles (160 km) across. It is hypothesized that one impact was so great it may have caused the dinosaurs to die out.

Could an asteroid endanger Earth today?

The rather unsettling answer is—maybe.

Until the early 19th century, astronomers thought the solar system was composed of just the Sun and a handful of planets. On New Year's Day in 1801, however, Italian astronomer Giuseppe Piazzi discovered an object between Jupiter and Mars that he first thought was a new comet—until subsequent observations revealed that it was moving in an orbit more like that of a small planet. Piazzi named it Ceres (now designated 1 Ceres, as it was the first asteroid to be discovered and have its orbit determined). Within a few years, similar

Asteroids may lurk in the icy Kuiper belt at the fringe of the solar system beyond Neptune, as shown in this artist's rendering.

bodies had been discovered and named. Since then, thousands have been discovered.

Asteroids, or minor planets, fall into several distinct groups, based on their positions in the solar system and their orbits. By far the largest number orbit in the main asteroid belt between Mars and Jupiter, at two to four times the distance from Earth to the Sun. They are believed to be fragments left over from the formation of the solar system that never coalesced into a planet. The largest is 1 Ceres; at some 550 miles (933 km) in diameter, it comprises about a quarter of the total mass of all the asteroids. Next largest are 2 Pallas, 4 Vesta, and 10 Hygiea, all of which are between 250 and 315 miles (400–525 km) in diameter. All the rest have a diameter of less than 200 miles (340 km). The mass of all known asteroids together is less than that of the Moon. All are rocky like the inner (terrestrial) planets; some are rocky and metallic (mainly with iron and nickel), showing signs of having melted from heat—mysterious, as all asteroids are too small to have evolved volcanoes.

Another group is the Trojan asteroids, which accompany Jupiter in its orbit—one group of several hundred clustered 60 degrees ahead of Jupiter, and another, somewhat smaller group

60 degrees behind. Thus, the two clusters of Trojan asteroids and Jupiter form an equilateral triangle in Jupiter's orbit.

There are also a few asteroids known as the Centaurs in the outer solar system, between Saturn and Uranus. They may be more icy than rocky, like the objects in the Kuiper belt. In fact, some of them are now believed to be comets rather than asteroids (in recent years, the distinction between asteroids and comets has been getting very fuzzy).

A few asteroids seem to be doing double duty as tiny moons circling the planets Mars, Jupiter, Saturn, Uranus, and Neptune—in the distant past having ventured so close to the planets that they were gravitationally captured into their orbits.

But the most intriguing group (for life on Earth) is the near-Earth asteroids—those whose orbits carry them particularly close to Earth, sometimes even well inside the orbit of the Moon! Some scientists speculate that the great explosion over the Tunguska forest in Siberia on June 30, 1908, might have been a small asteroid about 200 feet (60 m) in diameter. Trees were flattened across an area 30 miles (50 km) in diameter—several times larger than the area inside the Beltway around Washington, D.C. The object decelerated with the force of a modern nuclear warhead, about 10 megatons, but did not leave a crater because it disintegrated in midair. Scientists speculate that the asteroid was composed mostly of ice and other loose particles of rock that burned up in the atmosphere before reaching Earth's surface.

Astronomers estimate there are between 500 and 1,000 near-Earth asteroids larger than 0.6 miles (1 km) in diameter—big enough to cause global devastation if one struck Earth, principally by raising enough dust in the atmosphere to cool Earth's climate and disrupt agriculture worldwide. Since 1995, the National Aeronautics and Space Administration (NASA) in the United States has been operating the sensitive Near-Earth Asteroid Tracking (NEAT) camera in Hawaii. The task of NEAT and several other asteroid surveys is to discover and track all asteroids

The asteroid 243 Ida was photographed on August 28, 1993, by the *Galileo* spacecraft. *Galileo*'s images revealed that Ida has a small satellite called Dactyl (small spot to the lower right).

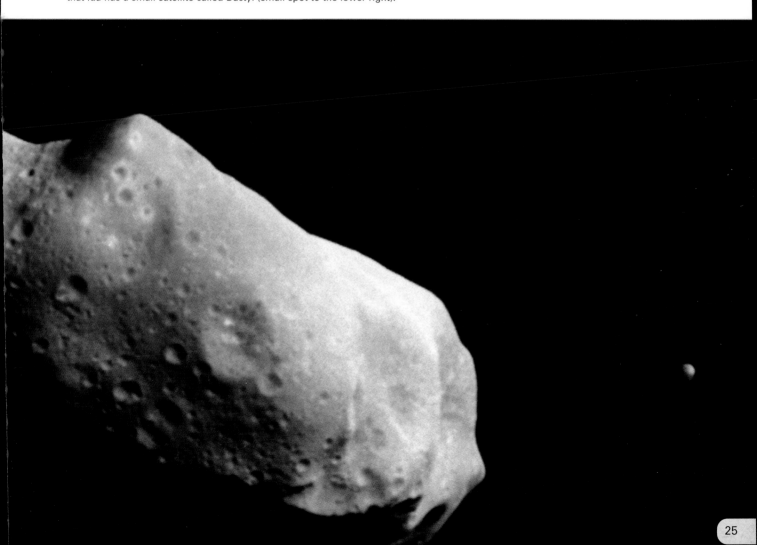

or comets that might pose a potential hazard to Earth—thereby giving scientists years, decades, or centuries to figure out how to deflect them.

Several asteroids have been visited by spacecraft. In 1993, the *Galileo* spacecraft (then on its way to Jupiter) swooped close by 243 Ida, a potato-shaped body measuring about 15 by 35 miles (23 by 58 km), and the photos it returned revealed a big surprise: Ida had its own natural satellite! Now named Dactyl, the remarkably round satellite is less than a mile (1.6 km) across and orbits Ida some 55 miles (90 km) away. The discovery of this pair has since led astronomers to find other binary asteroids in the main asteroid belt and among the near-Earth asteroids.

And in 2001, the *Near Earth Asteroid Rendezvous (NEAR) Shoemaker* spacecraft gently landed on 433 Eros, an even smaller asteroid believed to be a nearly pristine sample of the most ancient material in the solar system. Close-up photos showed that the surface of Eros appeared startlingly weathered, with peaks looking rounded and worn and craters filled with ponds of fine dust. Even more surprising, its surface was covered with loose boulders—astonishing to find on a body whose gravity is so weak that a basketball player would risk launching himself into orbit with a good jump shot!

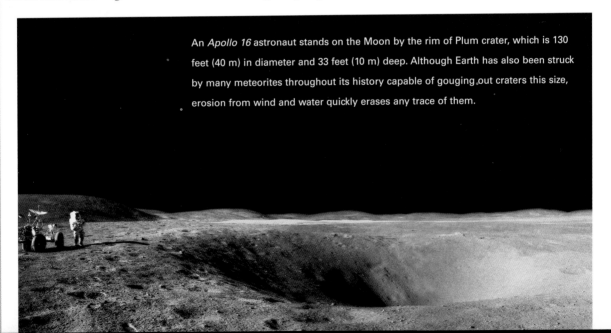

An *Apollo 16* astronaut stands on the Moon by the rim of Plum crater, which is 130 feet (40 m) in diameter and 33 feet (10 m) deep. Although Earth has also been struck by many meteorites throughout its history capable of gouging out craters this size, erosion from wind and water quickly erases any trace of them.

An artist's rendering depicting the catastrophic
impact of an asteroid striking Earth.

This photograph is a composite of four different negatives taken of the annual Leonid meteor shower in November 2001, capturing half a dozen meteors in eight minutes in partially cloudy skies over Joshua Tree National Park in California.

CHAPTER FOUR

Shooting Stars and Fireballs

In this five-minute time exposure photograph from Spruce Knob, West Virginia, on November 18, 2001, three Leonid meteors are shown shooting through skies near the constellation Orion.

During any night of the year, watch the nighttime star-spangled sky. Several times an hour, what looks like a star seems to fall from its position in the sky.

"Falling stars" or "shooting stars" are not stars at all but meteors—interplanetary sand and gravel speeding into Earth's atmosphere at 5 to 40 miles (10–70 km) per second. As they plow into the air, they incinerate themselves from the heat of friction with Earth's outer atmosphere 50 miles (80 km) overhead, glowing briefly as they burn away to nothing.

29

Earth's atmosphere is constantly bombarded by such interplanetary grains—about 100 tons (90 t) per day. That's the equivalent of 100 pickup trucks full of sand dumped into the air from space—each day! Most interplanetary specks are so microscopic that the meteors' light is too faint to be seen from the ground, even at night. Many brighter meteors from larger grains glow overhead during daylight, bright moonlight, or in bad weather, when their momentary light is obscured by the brilliance of the Sun or the Moon or is hidden by clouds. Even so, if one is vigilant, any night of the year a half-dozen so-called "sporadic meteors" an hour randomly streaking from different parts of the sky may be seen.

But certain nights are special. The solar system is ringed with concentrated collections of interplanetary sand and gravel (collectively called "meteoroids") orbiting the Sun—debris left behind by disintegrated comets. The orbits of about a dozen meteoroid streams intersect Earth's orbit where Earth happens to be on specific dates. Watch the starry sky on one of these dates for a meteor shower, when, depending on the shower, 20 to 50 or even more meteors an hour may streak across the sky.

Unlike sporadic meteors that whiz from any random direction, shower meteors appear to radiate from one small area of the sky, like droplets from a garden hose appear to spread out from the nozzle. Thus each known meteor shower is given the names of its radiant—the constellation from which the meteors appear to originate. One of the best annual shows is the Perseid meteor shower the second week of August, when 60 to 80 yellowish meteors as brilliant as the brightest stars or planets appear from the vicinity of the constellation Perseus and silently shoot halfway across the sky. One may even leave behind a faint train of smoke or that appear to explode silently at the end of its path. Another annual meteor shower that in some years has rained up to several thousand meteors per hour is the Geminids, appearing to radiate from the constellation Gemini during the second week of December.

If bits of interplanetary grit are constantly bombarding Earth's atmosphere, what about bigger chunks of rock?

Fortunately for Earth, by far most of the debris in interplanetary space is small—ranging in size from marbles down to fine sand. But every year or two, a chunk the size of a person's fist has come screaming into Earth's atmosphere. Streaking across the sky at tens of thousands of miles per hour, such a large object may briefly blaze brighter than the Moon or even the Sun, momentarily lighting the nighttime sky as bright as day. It may also sound a thunderclap of a sonic boom as the friction of the atmosphere slows it to the speed of sound, and it may leave a glowing, smokelike train that hangs aloft for minutes. Such fireballs (as brilliant meteors are called) have been seen night and day by anyone happening to look at the right moment.

This meteorite is composed of mostly iron and nickel and was found at Derrick Peak, Antarctica. This sample is most likely a small piece from the core of a large asteroid that broke apart.

Although even a suitcase-sized chunk of interplanetary debris is usually vaporized completely by the heat of the friction with Earth's protective atmosphere, a few times a century, fragments from even larger objects have made it all the way to the ground. Most meteorites (as they are called once they're on Earth) have landed in oceans, wilderness areas, or farmers' fields, but a few have struck houses or cars, and at least one has hit a person.

All in all, more than one million pounds (450 t) of meteorites have been found on Earth—some of them ancient, some of them actually seen to have fallen over the past three centuries. Nearly 80 percent of those are stony, similar to the mantles and crusts of the terrestrial planets. Nearly 20 percent are a combination of iron and nickel (some cultures—such as arctic peoples—fashioned knife blades and other tools from meteoritic iron). A few remaining meteorites are mixtures of iron and stony materials or are of a more unusual composition.

Truly large meteorites have scarred Earth with impact craters. One of the most famous—and youngest—is the Barringer Meteorite Crater in Arizona, three-quarters of a mile (1.2 km) across. It was created 20,000–50,000 years ago when an iron meteorite 100 to 150 feet (30–50 m) across blasted into Earth, releasing 10 to 100 megatons of energy—500 to 5,000 times the energy of the atomic bomb that was dropped on Hiroshima near the end of World War II. Astronomers calculate that such a massive meteorite might strike Earth every few thousand years.

All meteorites are treasured by astronomers and planetary geologists as precious samples from various

The Peekskill meteor of October 9, 1992, landed in Peekskill, New York, striking a car (both pictured here). The meteorite is composed of dense rock and has the size and mass of an extremely heavy bowling ball.

32

Barringer Meteorite Crater in the sandstone desert near Winslow, Arizona, resulted from an iron meteorite weighing several hundred thousand tons—about the mass of a freight train—striking Earth 20,000 to 50,000 years ago.

regions of the solar system—for from their chemical composition, it is clear that meteorites do not all come from one place. A few seem to have come from comets. Others appear to have come from the Moon or Mars, presumably material ejected when those bodies were bombarded by large chunks of interplanetary debris. Most meteorites, however, appear to come from asteroids—in fact, from their composition, it has even been possible to narrow down which asteroids.

Curtains of the aurora borealis or northern lights, which seem to be hovering wraithlike just above the trees, were actually 60 miles (100 km) or more above Earth. This photograph was taken in Heidmork, Iceland in February 2001.

CHAPTER FIVE

Dust, Particles, Fields, and Cosmic Light Shows

Not only does dust collect on the furniture in a house, but a vast cloud of it swirls around in the plane of the solar system. A good share of it is left over from the solar system's formation 4.5 billion years ago. But the dust is continually being replenished. Dust is left behind by dissipating comet tails, thrown off the Moon and planets when they're struck by meteoroids and asteroids, and shaken off asteroids when they've knocked together in the main asteroid belt.

Tiny cousins of meteoroids, interplanetary dust particles are as small as particles of smoke. But there's so much of the dust that it faintly reflects sunlight. Interplanetary dust can actually be seen if looked for on a moonless night from an exceptionally dark location.

With sensitive eyes and a dark location, one can see a faint glow stretching across the entire sky, from horizon to horizon, at an angle to the Milky Way—but much fainter than the Milky Way. This is the dust in the plane of the planets projected onto the sky. Because of the dust's reflective properties, however, parts of the band are brighter and easier to see than other parts and are thus seldom seen connected.

The most visible portion of the dust is the zodiacal light: a faint, triangular, whitish glow about as bright as the Milky Way, extending a third to halfway up the sky from the eastern or western horizon about two hours before sunrise and after sunset. Because of the geometry of the plane of Earth's orbit

In very dark, moonless skies at midnight, sunlight can be seen reflecting faintly off dust in interplanetary space. This faint, diffuse glow directly opposite the Sun is known as the *gegenschein* (German for "counter glow").

and that of its equator, the zodiacal light is best seen a couple of hours before sunrise in September and October (for a few weeks around the first day of autumn) and after sunset in March and April (for a few weeks around the first day of spring). It's surprisingly large and is sometimes called the false dawn, as it can be mistaken for early sunrise.

More challenging to see is the *gegenschein*, or "counter glow"—an exceptionally faint, round patch of light 20 to 30 times larger than a full Moon, which may be seen overhead at midnight, directly opposite the Sun. As it is much fainter than the zodiacal light, it must be looked for on a moonless night far away from city lights. The *gegenschein* is best seen in September and October, when it appears in a region of the sky far from the Milky Way.

In addition to microscopic dust, interplanetary space is also filled with even smaller particles: fragments of atoms. Flowing through the solar system are negatively charged electrons and positively charged nuclei from atoms of hydrogen, helium, and heavier elements—all thrown off by the Sun through the solar system as solar wind.

Zodiacal light, here seen above the western horizon from Kitt Peak National Observatory in Arizona in April 1977, is caused by sunlight scattering off interplanetary dust particles in orbit around the Sun. The short streaks are star trails from a long photographic exposure.

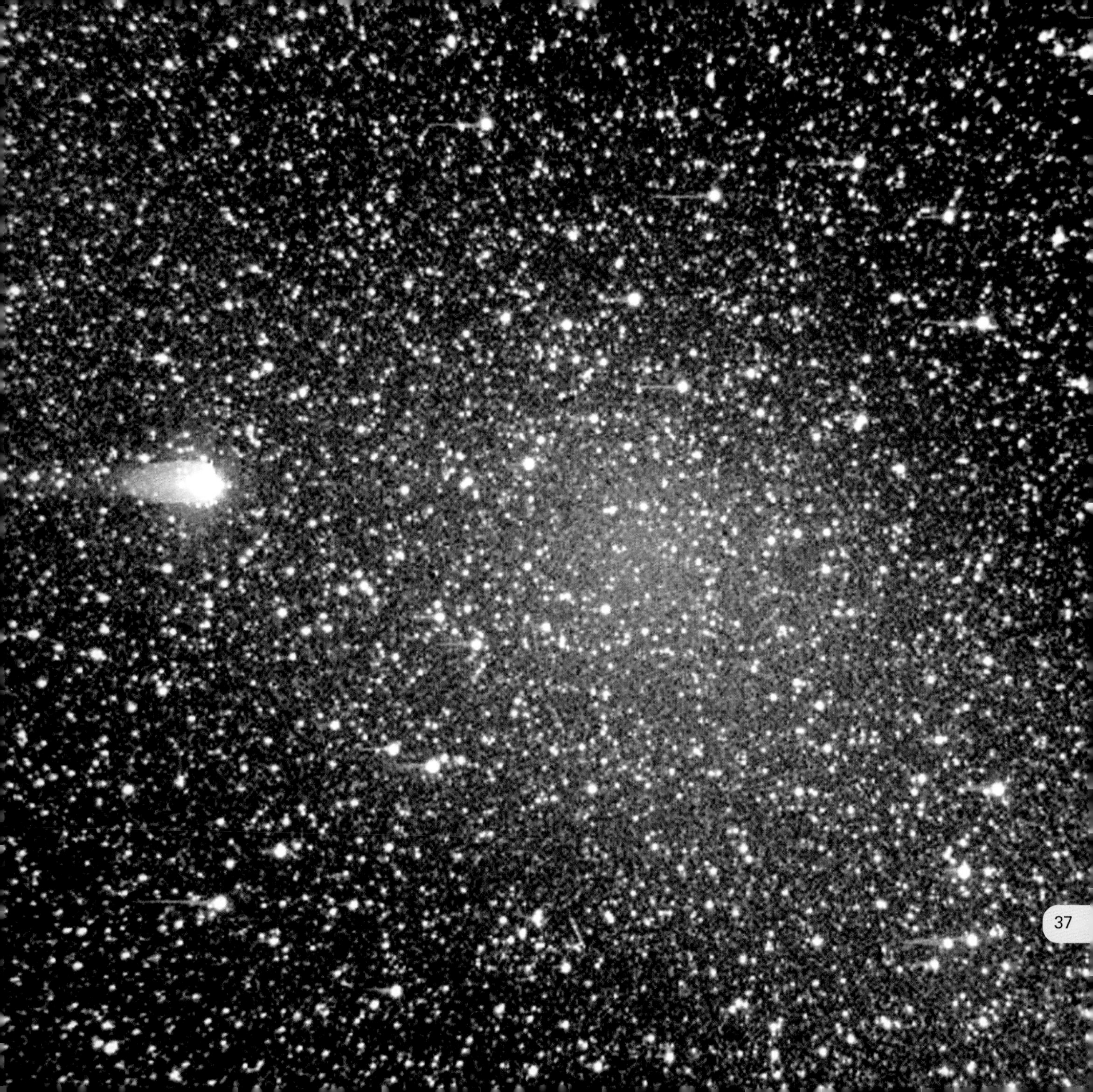

These charged solar particles—or, more accurately, their interactions with Earth's atmosphere—can be readily seen from a dark location, especially one at a very high northern or southern latitude, such as Canada or Australia.

How? Well, Earth is like a giant bar magnet, with magnetic field lines going into and out of its magnetic poles (close to the north and south poles of its axis of rotation). When charged particles encounter a magnetic field, they are guided past it as if by wires, spiraling around the magnetic field lines to the magnetic poles. So when the charged particles—mostly electrons—from the Sun reach Earth's magnetic field, they are accelerated toward Earth's poles and thus downward into Earth's atmosphere. And that's when the light show begins!

In Earth's extreme upper atmosphere, known as the ionosphere, 50 to 250 miles (80–400 km) overhead, the speeding charged particles collide violently with air atoms and molecules. The collisions energize the atoms and molecules, causing them to emit light and more electrons. The molecules start to glow like the gas in a neon sign, creating the lurid greens and reds of the flickering auroras, or northern and southern lights. The auroras' different colors are produced by different atoms: The characteristic yellow-green is usually produced by oxygen, whereas red often comes from nitrogen.

Auroras are most common and most spectacular during years when there are many sunspots on the face of the Sun—times when the Sun is also spewing out high numbers of charged particles. (Contact your local astronomy club, planetarium, or astronomical observatory for the current "space weather" prediction.) Also, the closer you are to the magnetic poles (for example, in Canada or Alaska), the better your chances of seeing auroras—although particularly energetic auroras have been seen even in the tropics.

Red aurora borealis, such as this one photographed from near Anchorage, Alaska, in 1977, are much rarer than green northern lights and are usually associated with exceptionally strong magnetic storms on the Sun.

The Milky Way—best seen from a truly dark site as a pale "highway" arcing across the nighttime sky—is actually the plane of our own galaxy. Viewed through binoculars or a telescope, its milky whorls reveal themselves to be thousands of stars, glowing gases, and dark lanes of dust.

Watching the Fireworks of Heaven

All that is needed to see the *gegenschein*, the zodiacal light, falling stars, auroras, and comet tails are unaided eyes (although binoculars can be nice for examining details). But the skies must be truly dark. Just how dark is dark? The average suburban backyard—from which only the brightest stars in the constellations can be seen and the night sky is always faintly illuminated by city lights—is simply not dark enough. Indeed, truly dark skies are becoming almost an endangered species in much of the world.

For ideal skies, a camping vacation should be planned for a year when the new moon falls close to the second week of August (many calendars show the phases of the moon). Drive far into a desert or hike in the mountains to a remote, primitive campsite where only tents (not RVs) are

Truly dark skies for stargazing can be a challenge to find, as shown by this experimental computer model of light pollution in the continental United States.

allowed so no electric lights burn all night. Set up camp away from a road to avoid headlights of passing cars. As the sky darkens after sunset, do not light candles or flashlights. Instead, lie back in a sleeping bag and let your eyes become fully accustomed to the deepening darkness. Within 45 minutes, the velvet-black sky will glitter breathtakingly with so many thousands of stars that it will be difficult to *find* well-known constellations, and the Milky Way will wind its way across the sky in full magnificence. Now several heavenly wonders put on by the smallest bodies in the solar system will be visible.

Watch the western sky above the horizon where the sun sets. An hour or two after sunset, a faint pyramid of whitish light whose apex (point) stretches toward the zenith, or highest point, will appear. That is the zodiacal light—light reflected from dust grains in interplanetary space. Watch for it also above the eastern horizon an hour or two before sunrise.

Around midnight, look for what may seem to be a rather large, isolated patch of faint light—almost like a detached part of the Milky Way—more or less directly overhead. That's the *gegenschein*. Both the zodiacal light and the *gegenschein* are so low-contrast that they're best viewed with the unaided eye.

Also around midnight in August, when the constellation Perseus is rising, a bright shooting star may streak halfway across the night sky, maybe followed a minute or two later by another. . .and another. Those are meteors, grains of sand and dust plunging into Earth's atmosphere. The annual Perseid meteor shower, which peaks between August 10 and 14 each year, is reliably one of the best annual meteor showers. Usually the Perseids are as bright as the brightest stars and planets in the sky, long, slow, and yellowish; some of the brightest ones may even leave faint glowing trains! Again, meteors are best observed with the naked eye.

(As an extra activity, microscopic meteorites can be collected on the roof of one's house. Best are tile roofs, since they drain well and don't produce other particles or debris. Place a deep bowl at the base of a drain spout when a rainstorm is predicted. After the storm, remove leaves and other large debris, carefully pour out most of the water, and allow the rest of the material to dry thoroughly. Shake the dried

Meteor showers put on a gorgeous show a dozen times a year as Earth travels through streams of dust particles left behind by disintegrated comets. Because the dust particles are traveling in parallel paths in space, to an observer on Earth they will appear to radiate from one point in the sky. This radiant point is a perspective effect, rather like railroad tracks receding into the distance appear to vanish at one point on the horizon.

Generally, meteor showers are named after the constellation in which their radiant falls at the time the shower reaches its maximum. The table below lists the peak days of major showers (not included are additional minor showers, such as the Alpha Capricornids from July 30–August 1). It's worth watching a day or two earlier and later, though, as most showers last for a few days to a week.

As the table dramatically reveals, you'll see the most showers from a dark site away from city lights on cloudless nights with no moonlight. (Zenithal Hourly Rate is the predicted maximum number of falling stars you would see if the radiant were directly overhead.)

Four different rates are given for each shower, under the following conditions:

1. city sky or rural sky with full Moon
2. suburb sky or rural sky with quarter Moon
3. rural sky and Moonless
4. calculated Zenith Hourly Rate (ZHR)

Date	Shower	Rates: (1)	(2)	(3)	(4)
Jan 3–4	Quadrantids	5	10	25	120
Apr 21–22	April Lyrids	4	7	15	15
May 4–5	Eta Aquarids	4	6	10	40
Jul 28–29	Delta Aquarids	4	7	15	20
Aug 12–13	Perseids	10	20	40	120
Oct 21–22	Orionids	5	10	25	25
Nov 3–13	Taurids	4	6	10	10
Nov 16–17	Leonids	5	10	15	15
Dec 13–14	Geminids	18	35	85	85
Dec 21–22	Ursids	3	5	10	20

material onto a sheet of paper and hold a magnet under the paper; then gently tilt and tap the paper so that most of the nonmagnetic particles fall off. A few of the remaining magnetic particles will likely be iron micrometeorites, which are identifiable under a microscope as rounded and perhaps pitted from partially melting in their fiery journey through the atmosphere.)

Whether or not an aurora is visible will depend not only on the darkness of the skies but also on the latitude (the latitude of Canada or Alaska is ideal) and the activity of the sun—the more sunspots and flares on the sun, the more auroras on Earth. A local astronomy club, planetarium, or observatory will know. There are also Web sites that keep track of sunspots and "space weather."

Seeing a comet will also depend on whether one is in the vicinity of the inner solar system; bright comets visible to the unaided eye are frequently written up in daily newspapers.

For spotting Pluto, asteroids, and faint objects in the Kuiper belt and the Oort cloud, a good-sized telescope is needed—again, the best place to start is a local astronomy club, a planetarium, or an observatory with public observing nights. (The monthly magazines *Astronomy* and *Sky & Telescope* also feature advertisements of commercial companies selling telescopes of various sizes.)

Happy observing!

This photograph, taken in April 1997 with a fisheye lens, captures much of the spectacle that may be available for viewing in the night sky. Comet Hale-Bopp blazes to the right of center, its tail pointing directly away from the setting Sun. Also captured in this single frame are thousands of stars, several constellations, a trace of zodiacal light, and the planet Mercury, rising just over the horizon.

Further Information

Beatty, J. Kelly, "NEAR Falls for Eros," *Sky & Telescope*, vol. 101. No. 5, pp. 34–37 (May 2001).

Beatty, J. Kelly, Carolyn Collins Petersen, and Andrew Chaikin (editors), *The New Solar System* (fourth edition, Sky Publishing Co. and Cambridge University Press, 1999).

Burtnyk, Kimberly, "Anatomy of an Aurora," *Sky & Telescope*, vol. 99, no. 3, pp. 34–40 (March 2000).

Eather, Robert H., "An Aurora Watcher's Guide," *Sky & Telescope*, vol. 99, no. 3, pp. 42–48 (March 2000).

Gupta, Rajiv, *Observer's Handbook*, The Royal Astronomical Society of Canada, (University of Toronto Press, published annually).

Levy, David H. (editor), *The Scientific American Book of the Cosmos* (St. Martin's Press, 2000).

O'Meara, Stephen James, "Seeking the Elusive Gegenschein," *Sky & Telescope,* vol. 100, no. 4, pp. 116–119 (October 2000).

American Meteor Society (for amateur observers in the United States), www.amsmeteors.org

Home page for "The Nine Planets: A Multimedia Tour of the Solar System" http://seds.lpl.arizona.edu/nineplanets/nineplanets/nineplanets.html

International Meteor Organization (for amateur observers outside the United States), www.imo.net

International Occultation Timing Association (IOTA) (for amateur observers interested in timing eclipses of stars by asteroids), http://www.lunar-occultations.com/iota/iotandx.htm

Views of the Solar System photo archive index page for asteroids, comets, Kuiper belt, meteorites, Oort cloud, and Pluto http://www.solarviews.com/cap/index

Glossary

asteroid—A minor planet or chunk of rock ranging from less than half a mile (1 km) to 550 miles (900 km) in diameter orbiting the Sun; most asteroids orbit between Mars and Jupiter, but some have other orbits—including some that nearly approach Earth.

aurora—The red and green "northern lights" (aurora borealis) frequently seen at high northern latitudes (and at high southern latitudes, as the aurora australis, or "southern lights") when charged particles from the Sun interact with Earth's magnetic field and atmosphere.

coma—The cloud of gas surrounding the nucleus of a comet.

comet—A mountain-sized "dirty snowball" (a chunk of ice and rocky material) in orbit around the Sun that can grow tails up to several hundred million miles long when it is heated in approaching the Sun.

dust tail—The curved, whitish cometary tail produced by grains of dust pushed away from a comet's nucleus by solar wind.

fireball—A meteor roughly brighter than the planet Venus (the brightest planet in the sky).

gegenschein—A faint whitish glow appearing roughly overhead at midnight that is produced by sunlight reflecting off interplanetary dust.

ion tail—The straight, bluish cometary tail produced by charged subatomic particles pushed away from a comet's nucleus by the radiation pressure of sunlight.

ionosphere—A very tenuous layer of Earth's upper atmosphere several hundred miles high where auroras are produced.

Kuiper belt—A region beyond the planet Neptune populated by icy, asteroid-like worldlets and believed to be the birthplace of short-period comets.

long-period comet—A comet that approaches the Sun less often than once every 200 years.

meteor—A streak of light, often called a "falling" or "shooting" star, produced when a sand- or gravel-sized grain of interplanetary material plunges into Earth's atmosphere and glows from the heat of friction with air molecules.

meteorite—A stony or iron chunk of material on Earth that came from interplanetary space.

meteoroids—Grains of sand and gravel in interplanetary space before they plunge into Earth's atmosphere; believed to be the debris left by a disintegrated comet.

meteor shower—A "rain" of meteors seen several times a year, occurring when Earth passes through a stream of meteoroids.

nucleus, cometary—The solid main body of a comet.

Oort cloud—A spherical halo surrounding the solar system and extending as far as $\frac{1}{10}$ of the way to the nearest star, populated by icy, asteroid-like worldlets and believed to be the birthplace of long-period comets.

perihelion—The point in a body's orbit at which it passes closest to the Sun.

short-period comet—A comet that approaches the Sun more often than once every 200 years.

sonic boom—The thunderclap-type sound produced when a body "goes through the sound barrier"—that is, passes through the speed of sound in Earth's atmosphere.

sporadic meteors—Meteors coming from random directions through the atmosphere, not associated with a stream of meteoroids that gives rise to a meteor shower.

zodiacal light—A faint whitish glow visible in the west about two hours after sunset and in the east about two hours before sunrise, produced by sunlight reflecting off interplanetary dust.

Index